REA

FRIENDS OF ACPL

SO-EPD-645

242 C36i
Chaney, Robert Galen, 1913-
The inner way

THE INNER WAY

by
ROBERT GALEN CHANEY

For those who seek the Light—

ASTARA'S LIBRARY OF MYSTICAL CLASSICS
800 WEST ARROW HIGHWAY
P.O. BOX 5003
UPLAND, CALIFORNIA 91785

Copyright, 1962
by
Robert Galen Chaney
Library of Congress 75-32234
ISBN 0-918936-00-4
Fourth Edition, 1987

Printed in the United States of America by—
Ideal Printing Company, City of Industry, CA

To
Maree F. Chaney,
my mother

THE INNER WAY

PREFACE

This book has been written specially for anyone whose life is full . . . crammed, in fact, with many things to do, many problems to meet, and little time for leisurely contemplation. It is written for him who must "read while he runs."

Having been just such a person for nearly half a century, I know from personal experience that some of life's most fruitful moments are not in the frenzied outer world but in the calm inner world. The inner moments have provided me with whatever talents I possess for coping with difficult situations and developing any inspirational qualities I have acquired as a lecturer and writer.

It was Goethe who suggested that character is built in crowds but talents grow in solitude. This is particularly true of the talent for meeting life's problems, for maintaining poise in the face of trials and afflictions, for gaining cherished goals, or just for meeting life's everyday tensions. We seldom have time for the strengthening solitude, however; hence, this book. It is to help you organize and make the most productive use of any quiet moments available.

In short, this book is for you . . . if you have a problem and if you are in a hurry.

Robert Galen Chaney

CONTENTS

PREFACE 9

PRACTICE THE POWERFUL SILENCE 15

THE INNER WAY TO A NEW LIFE 26

ACQUIRE STRENGTH, CONFIDENCE AND PEACE 38
    The inner way to strength 42
    The inner way to confidence 44
    The inner way to peace of mind 46

THE TRIANGLE OF HEALTH— BODY, MIND AND SPIRIT 48
    The inner way to heal your body 52
    The inner way to heal your mind 54
    The inner way to release tension 56

THE INNER WAY

THE ONE RULE FOR A NEW LIFE 58
    The inner way to stabilize your life 62
    The inner way to improve your life 64
    The inner way to material progress 66

EMPHASIZE YOUR BEST QUALITIES 68
    The inner way to right decisions 72
    The inner way to develop your talents
    and skills 74
    The inner way to enhance your personality 76

THE OPEN DOOR TO THE FATHER'S HOUSE.. 78
    The inner way to contact the Infinite 82
    The inner way to the power of the Infinite 84
    The inner way to the great source of life .. 86

THE INNER WAY

CREATIVE COOPERATION WITH THE INFINITE 88
    The inner way to creative work 92
    The inner way to creative ideas 94
    The inner way to creative self-expression.. 96

ORGANIZE YOUR INNER LIFE 98
    The inner way to order 102
    The inner way to harmony 104
    The inner way to serenity 106

FEEL THE DYNAMIC PRESENCE 108
    The inner way to the Infinite Presence 112
    The inner way to let God act through you..114
    The inner way to receive the dynamic Infinite Spirit 116

THE INNER WAY

THE KEY TO YOUR DESIRES 118
    The inner way to success in business 122
    The inner way to success in personal relationships 124
    The inner way to success in spiritual growth 126

TAP THE ETERNAL RESOURCES 128
    The inner way to mental alertness 132
    The inner way to physical strength 134
    The inner way to emotional stability 136

MAKE YOUR LIFE PRODUCTIVE 138
    The inner way to improve your memory 142
    The inner way to gain important goals 144
    The inner way to awaken the whole person..146

PRACTICE THE POWERFUL SILENCE

There was once a speaker who wrote his lectures in advance and included marginal notes to remind himself of appropriate gestures and tone of voice. He frequently made the note, "Not very interesting here. Wave arms and talk loud."

The story is fictitious. But the point it illustrates is tragically true.

There are many people in the world who make a great deal of noise. You have seen them in all areas of life: in international affairs, in business, and among your friends.

THE INNER WAY

As a rule, the weaker the logic the greater the noise.

Little people chatter and clatter. Big people exert power quietly. The expert swimmer never makes a big splash.

It seems a peculiarity of human nature that weakness blusters while strength is serene. Is it not possible, however, that this is more than merely a psychological facet of the human personality?

Throughout man's long history the great works of literature and art have originated in the powerful silence of the inner mind . . . the mind detached, momentarily at least, from the din of the outer world. The original channel for the creation of every religion received the spiritual impulse or religious experience in solitary inwardness.

THE INNER WAY

And now, studies in modern scientific research, comparing scientists working alone on a problem with those working in groups on the same problem, show that the scientist working alone not only makes more discoveries he also makes better ones!

The logical conclusion, then, is that you may seek the group or community for social and commercial enterprises. But for personal aspiration and realization, the solution of problems, and the creative shouldering of responsibility and crisis, you will succeed or fail on your own efforts.

And yet, this is not entirely true. There is a way . . . a solitary way . . . an inner way . . . through which you can form a productive association with what, for lack of a better term, we will designate as *the Infinite*.

You will have your own personal meaning for this term, the Infinite. To you it may mean God . . . as a Person, or an unpersonified Being, or an all-pervading Essence, or a form of Cosmic Consciousness. You may give it any one of the thousand names men have assigned it. Or you may not even consider the Infinite as a Supreme Being at all, but as some electronic conglomerate of basic force and knowledge.

Your precise understanding of the Infinite is a personal matter with you and in no way alters the objective of this book, which is to help you form a productive, personal, association with it. Whatever your concept of the term may be, the

THE INNER WAY

Infinite constitutes a unique Quality with which you may become associated . . . and through which association you may accomplish some remarkable alterations in your life.

It is but ordinary logic that man's physical body functions best when provided natural, uncontaminated food. Insofar as you possibly can, you avoid polluting your physical system with unnatural substances which damage your body. And you probably supplement your diet with natural vitamins which provide an extra spark of physical energy.

But can the same be said of your mental nourishment? Must your mind forever struggle with the impure mental diet which life so frequently provides? Or will you

THE INNER WAY

give it the opportunity to receive the higher sustenance which will nourish and strengthen? The manna from heaven is the food which the Infinite provides. There is a way for you to obtain this higher substance.

Perhaps you have never realized that you possess a little used faculty of mind which can change your life completely.

This faculty can enable you to meet your problems successfully. It can help you withstand trials and troubles and overcome worry. It can improve your relationships with others. It can even help you become more successful.

It is simple to use, yet it requires self-discipline. It has been known for ages, yet its great secret is that you must discover it for yourself. It bears a kinship to your faculty of imaginative creativity, yet it is a decidedly higher attribute.

This remarkable faculty is your *sense* of intimate and productive association with the Infinite.

The prime purpose of these pages is to help you discover and develop this superior sense faculty.

This faculty is considerably more than imagination; it is *life-intuition*. And if you make the attempt you will develop a response to it which will charge your entire being with a new life, a greater vitality, a keen alertness of mind, a surprising strength and forcefulness.

Like any faculty it must be used to be developed and strengthened. You must practice to become proficient with it. The

THE INNER WAY

Infinite, though indwelling, is distant until you make it intimate. And here is the inner way to do it.

Arrange your life to include not less than five minutes each day, and certainly more if possible, for the act of personal, inner identification with the Infinite. This is especially essential when you are faced with a problem, a sorrow, a discouraging circumstance of any kind.

From the inner attunement aids . . . the inner ways . . . given later in this book select the one which most definitely applies to your greatest need of the moment. This will vary from time to time with changing circumstances, needs and desires.

Read the attunement aid slowly. Completely assimilate the meaning of each sen-

THE INNER WAY

tence. Savor the taste of its mental and emotional flavor.

When you come to the symbol ¶, pause a few moments. Be still. Close your eyes and ears to the world around you. Center your attention upon your breathing until it becomes slow and rhythmic.

Then reflect upon the thought you have read before going on to the next attunement. Try to *feel* its meaning inwardly.

Let its personal significance flow through your mind. Let it become as an actual substance which fills your entire being with a new strength and spirit.

What you are attempting to do is inwardly feel or sense the presence and power of the Infinite and all its attributes.

Do this regularly each day. Two or three

times each day if possible, but at least once without fail. Engage in this activity whenever you can arrange a brief quiet moment.

In a surprisingly short time you will discover that you can quickly go to the Inner Way even in your busiest seconds. Inner quietness and identification with the Infinite is possible even in the midst of outer din.

In this simple but effective manner you travel the Inner Way to a new and better life. This is how you conquer through quietness. This is how quietness brings power where noise and busyness dissipate strength. This is the way to practice the powerful silence.

Now let us see whether or not the Inner Way may be related to your busy life.

THE INNER WAY

Let us see what it can accomplish for you. If it is not practical it is valueless. Let us see if it can be applied to the real problems of real people.

THE INNER WAY
TO A NEW LIFE

Swirling around me as this is written is the never ending flow of people with problems. I am in the Los Angeles International Airport, in the waiting room of a huge airline.

Here is a cross section of this pulsing, impatient world, crowded with people hurrying to or from life's important matters. Business, illness, life and death, intimate personal situations, dreams and aspirations and the precarious state of the world are constantly thrusting problems into their lives.

At random I interrupt with, "Pardon me,

THE INNER WAY

please. I am making a survey of personal problems. Will you help me?"

This introduction enabled me to visit on common ground with the wealthy and the poor, with people of different hues of skin and different shades of belief, with businessmen and housewives, with native sons and daughters and residents of other lands. They have freely given me their personal opinions of the problems man faces.

Of them all, only one man believed that the individual's problems could be solved by changing world conditions. He was a university administrator who literally refused to discuss anything with me until he was assured I actually had attended a university also. He then became willing to express his opinions which included: man's only problem is insecurity, which can be solved by social change; the "masses" are stupid; all spiritual experience is only psychological; religion is "poppycock" and a "crutch" for the ignorant.

As I left him to visit with another, I had the feeling that he was the only really insecure person I had talked with all that day.

With this one exception, every person with whom I visited said that problems must be approached, and solved if possible, from within the individual himself. Is there a more clearly expressed validation of the Inner Way as your greatest opportunity for an enriched life?

The concensus of opinions among these

wayfarers was that there were five principal problems:

> Loneliness
> Grief over death of a loved one
> Unhappy marital relationship
> Loss of employment
> Incurable illness

Of course there were many other problems which do not fall precisely under these headings. And the importance of a problem varied greatly depending upon the individual's age and circumstances. A problem at one age is not a problem at another. A serious problem in one circumstance may be merely an annoyance in another.

Some of these problems seem to have easy solutions and some have not. Frequently the nature of an individual determines whether a solution may be arrived at or not. Sometimes the nature of a problem makes a solution impossible.

Whatever the circumstance and the nature of your problem, it is possible for you to meet it with both greater understanding and fortitude, and in many instances to solve it, if you will avail yourself of the benefits of the Inner Way.

In most persons there seethes an inner war. Personal psychological conflicts destroy more lives and dissipate more talents than the wars of men against men ever have. Man against himself is the true tyrant.

It may be safe to say that 999 of every thousand persons never live their full potential because of what happens or does not happen within themselves. For most persons "the battle of life" is an appropriate term. And unfortunately it is reflected outwardly in acts of hostility (often unconscious) that destroy personal associations, opportunities and even one's own physical self.

The Inner Way, properly pursued, creates a unique effect upon the nature of the one who follows it. The only words which even approach describing this result, although they are not at all adequate, are the words *Inner Transformation*.

Is a transformation of the inner being worthwhile? In truth it is the priceless quality which brings peace to the inner war and productiveness to the outer life.

An inner transformation achieved as a result of your inwardly dealing with a problem is one of the most gratifying of all experiences. It may take many turns. It may:

> enable you to solve your problem,
> give you the fortitude to withstand it if it cannot be solved,
> enable you to discover there is no problem, or
> enable you to arrange your life so the problem disappears, or no longer matters.

The persons with whom I visited believed that religion as an organized agency cannot solve your problem. It can offer suggestions that may, or may not, be of help. But the sum of their opinions was that only you can solve your problem. Another emphatic exhortation to try the Inner Way.

An interesting sidelight which appeared

from visiting with these sojourning problem solvers relates to the doctrine of exclusiveness . . . that its particular religion is the only valid one . . . which is the claim of nearly every organized religion. With but two exceptions, and remember these people were from many religious backgrounds, they believed this claim was folly and nonspiritual on its very surface.

Inner transformation, obviously, may occur in a follower of any religion . . . or a follower of none.

So it appears that this inner way of problem-solving, or living a more productive life, is available to you whatever your belief, nationality or race. The spiritual activity is completely *impersonal* in that it does not distinguish between you and anyone else. It is absolutely *personal* in that it functions in you separately from everyone else. And it is *universal* in that it functions in everyone to some degree, or may do so, however slight in many instances.

To paraphrase the words of one great spiritual teacher, "the problems are always with you." Life is a constant substituting of one problem, or set of problems, for another. It is not the purpose of this book to contend that for each problem there is a specific solution. You are not an electronic data computer into which can be fed a problem and out of which, a few seconds later, arrives a ready-made remedy. You are a human being encountering situations which are completely different from those in the lives of other human beings.

THE INNER WAY

You may be individuated from the Infinite, but you are not detached from it. You change yourself both inwardly and outwardly when you discover the point of attachment. Within you is the means of activating the connection which transforms . . . the point of contact with greater dimensions of wisdom and power, your identification with the Infinite.

In this book I do not offer you a religion with a name and creed and form. Nor a religion housed in marble or overlaid with gold leaf. Nor, actually, any religion at all. Yet it is all religions in one.

This Inner Way is the substance of which all religions in their pure and original form are created. It is also the material of which successful lives are made. This is the work of the craftsman who transforms a rough slab of stone or piece of wood into a thing of beauty. This is the mortar which holds in bond the temple not made with hands, eternal in the heaven of your consciousness. This is the *personal spiritual act,* the Inner Way, which creates an inner transformation.

THE INNER WAY

REMEMBER—

Among the attunement aids which follow, each day select the one which most definitely applies to your greatest need of the moment.

Read the attunement aid slowly. Completely assimilate the meaning of each sentence.

At each symbol ¶, pause . . . be still . . . try to *feel* its meaning inwardly. Let this *feeling* fill your entire being with a new strength and spirit.

You are sensing the presence and power of the Infinite and all its attributes. You are traveling the Inner Way to a new and greater life.

You are enabling the Infinite to function in and through you and every circumstance of your life.

THE INNER WAY

ACQUIRE STRENGTH, CONFIDENCE AND PEACE

This is not a book about what others have experienced. It is about what you can experience... and accomplish.

In the maelstrom of life you may have encountered swirling eddies of doubt, despair and sorrow. However difficult they are, it is possible for you to acquire the inner fortitude to withstand them and find the inner peace of life's calmer currents.

If you are momentarily trapped by one or more of these whirlpools you may free yourself through inner association with the divine qualities of confidence, poise and stability. You may overcome any present con-

THE INNER WAY

fusion, despair or sorrow and gird yourself with an unyielding inner amor which no ordeal can penetrate.

But you must find and generate the essential inner qualities . . . not only in the inner depths of your being, but more importantly in your unique faculty of attunement with the Great Source of all life and every one of its attributes. You must go to that inner place where hopelessness does not exist. You must seek that point which is beyond space and time and the world of material things . . . hidden deep in your consciousness where it awaits that sublime moment when you free it to function in every aspect of your life.

There is a time-honored way to discover this hallowed inner place of light, of release from the problems of your life. It is a way which floods the outer darkness with the inner light. It is a way which enables you to face the world and its perplexities with confidence, even boldness.

It is the way which the saints, sages and mystics of all times, peoples and religions discovered as the only method of overcoming their own frailties and of meeting the aggressions which others directed against them. Without exception they used it to surmount their apparently overwhelming difficulties.

They discovered that outer things . . . wealth, power, possessions . . . mean little in the face of trouble. They developed, every one of them, that special sense faculty which actively united them with life's most stalwart forces.

THE INNER WAY

The one way is the Inner Way.

As you interiorize your point of active consciousness you begin to work a miracle in your own nature. Its outer superficialities begin to drop away. Spirited buds of life appear. Fresh with inner vigor and eternal vitality they herald the new person which you are becoming.

The inner attunement aids which follow will help you accomplish the pleasant task of arousing to its highest effectiveness every divine spark of confidence, poise and stability which lies dormant within you. Be still then. Momentarily penetrate the veil which encloses the inner holy of holies. Let the potencies of your true spiritual Self begin to express themselves.

THE INNER WAY

The Inner Way to Strength

When your body is at rest, and your mind at peace, and when nothing of the surrounding world claims your attention . . . then interior spiritual processes begin to function.

It is then that your mind becomes attuned with Infinite Mind. Your higher nature is freed from its physical limitations and begins to express itself in your life. Every segment of your life yields to this spiritualizing and strengthening influence.

Inner receptive faculties receive emanations from the God-source of all life, and work their irresistible expressions therein.

THE INNER WAY

To increase their supply and their effectiveness, hold these thoughts in your mind as you turn to the Inner Way:

In my consciousness I create a state of receptivity to the God-force that surrounds me and permeates my being at this moment—¶

This Supreme Power, directed to my personal needs, reaches into every situation in my life—¶

It harmonizes . . . it calms . . . it opens new ways . . . it strengthens—¶

I am in the Infinite Light, and the Infinite Light is in me—¶

THE INNER WAY

The Inner Way to Confidence

For a moment, put aside your association with the world of people and things and take up your association with the inner world. Disconnect the senses which insistently inform of the world around you. Intensify the senses which alert your awareness of the world within you.

Through this inner, higher world you become associated with elements which know no fear or lack of faith. You become permeated with an aura of assurance and positiveness. These qualities become permanently fixed in your nature.

The deeper you turn inwardly the greater your awareness of the inner and higher

THE INNER WAY

world. Your realization of its effectiveness in your life is heightened. The more indelibly this Kingdom of God is etched upon your consciousness the more influence does it exert upon your life.

Let your mind become attuned to these thoughts:

> *Awareness of the physical world disappears from my consciousness—¶*
>
> *In the deepest quietness of my being I find myself touching a higher life—¶*
>
> *The peace, the harmony and the strength of that higher life become a part of my life—¶*
>
> *I am in the Infinite Light, and the Infinite Light is in me—¶*

THE INNER WAY

The Inner Way to Peace of Mind

At the inner center of your being is a Place of Light. This is where you meet with the Infinite.

Take a moment to comprehend the inner Light. Let it become so radiant a part of your life that it glows even in your darkest moments. Each time you do this the Light grows stronger and every portion of your life is soothed and uplifted by its rays.

Accord a welcome entry to the Infinite Spirit as it enters the gate of your consciousness. It brings more Light. It dissipates the shadows which your mind normally entertains. It diffuses through your mind into every phase of your life.

Open the Inner Way. Become inwardly receptive. Be joyful within . . . and at peace.

Direct your mind to consider these thoughts:

I am receiving the Infinite Spirit into my being and my life—¶

It fills me with Light . . . with understanding . . . with love—¶

It soothes and heals and fills me with peace—¶

It implants the Spiritual Essence in every activity of my life—¶

I am in the Infinite Light, and the Infinite Light is in me—¶

THE TRIANGLE OF HEALTH— BODY, MIND AND SPIRIT

None of the ills which beset mind, body or spirit are permanent. And every one of them may be healed.

The effectiveness of whatever means of healing you prefer . . . medicine, surgery, psychiatry, manipulation, nature cures or powerful faith . . . may be heightened by your use of the Inner Way. It adds that indefinable quality which tips the balance away from ill health and misery and toward a hygeia of all life.

A famous surgeon was seen praying prior to an extremely delicate operation. He was asked why he did so when he was so com-

THE INNER WAY

petent and skilled in his own right. He replied, "I cannot tell where my efforts end and God's begin."

Use any method of healing you desire . . . but never neglect the Inner Way that allows life's higher agencies to contribute their influence.

Mind, body and spirit . . . all three react to influences higher and more effective than you realize. Jung, the famous psychiatrist, said that none of his patients were healed unless they implanted a vital religious influence in their minds. There is hardly a physician in the world who has not witnessed healings of apparently hopeless cases . . . healings which were not accomplished by his ministrations, however expert, but which apparently yielded to some force higher than those which he normally wields.

Pain, whether physical, emotional or mental, increases wherever tension exists. When bodily and mental functions are forced to struggle against tension as well as an illness, they are encumbered with a double duty to perform. Their effectiveness is decreased by one half.

Whatever you do to release tension in the face of illness and pain frees all the miraculous curative powers, which nature has already provided you, to contribute their efforts toward healing. There is little in the outer world which will relieve tension as effectively as the Inner Way. Unlike many drugs it presents no undesirable side or after effects. It may be used

THE INNER WAY

even while you are engaged in other activities, provided you have frequently practiced it in times of seclusion and quietness.

Some have discovered that the faculty of imagination helps relieve tension. Visualize yourself floating on a soft, billowy cloud, or surrounded and permeated by a soothing sphere of light.

Deep breathing is also calming and tension releasing. A few slow deep breaths before engaging in any of the attunement aids which follow will increase their effectiveness immeasurably.

Confronted with pain, with any type of illness, achieve calmness and certainty by traveling the Inner Way. It refreshes. It relieves tension. It soothes and heals.

THE INNER WAY

The Inner Way to Heal Your Body

The physical house in which you live may be conditioned by the spiritual domain of which you are a part. The spiritual world acts upon your material world according to your direction.

Begin now to relate the lower to the higher. Consciously ask that the higher become more fully involved with the lower. Consciously direct the spiritual into those specific areas of your material, physical world wherein a harmonizing and healing influence is necessary.

Let there be an easing of the inner tensions which disrupt the flow of spirituality into the situations of your life. Let there

THE INNER WAY

be a radiating of the spiritualizing influence through you, as a focal point, into any pain or illness or any other disturbing situation in your life.

To activate this process, center your mind on these ideas:

> *The world of matter and form is influenced by my mind, my will, as the directive agencies of spiritual power—¶*
>
> *My mind and will direct the world of spiritual power to exert its influence in my body—¶*
>
> *I direct that spiritual power to deliver its essence, its harmony and strength, into my body—¶*
>
> *I am in the Infinite Light,
> and the Infinite Light is in me—¶*

THE INNER WAY

The Inner Way to Heal Your Mind

The deepest of your yearnings, the highest of your aspirations, may be strengthened by Infinite Power. When disturbances of mind and emotion are brought under the influence of that Power they, too, yield to its influence.

Create in your consciousness a realization that you partake of the substance of God . . . that you are a part of the Being of God . . . that, when you allow them to do so, superior influences will calm and stabilize your mind and emotions.

You are simply activating an awareness of what you really are. And through that state of heightened awareness and perception a new realization enters your consciousnss. The firm realization of your Self as a being of Light . . . a being of Power . . . and a being with a Purpose.

Orient your mind so that it dwells on these thoughts:

> *I am a center of consciousness through which the Infinite Consciousness is manifest—¶*
>
> *I am a center of orderly action through which Infinite Will is expressed—¶*
>
> *I am a center of harmony in which Infinite Love resides—¶*
>
> *I am in the Infinite Light, and the Infinite Light is in me—¶*

THE INNER WAY

The Inner Way to Release Tension

In the Supreme Being there is no tension. There is a stable, constant expression of will and purpose . . . but there is no tension.

It will help you release your own tensions if you can realize that you are as much a part of that Supreme Being as anyone or anything in the universe. To feel your inner connection with the Supreme Being is to convert His stability and constancy into your own being.

For a moment, therefore, inwardly sense your union with God. Through the Inner Way begin to know Him in consciousness, in essence, in reality, in inner substance.

Inwardly *feel* the meaning of the words, "I am in the Father, and the Father is in me." Spiritual teachers of every religion have made this statement and found it to be as true of other persons as of themselves. Repeat this statement several times as a directive to your consciousness.

Let your mind become centered upon these thoughts:

> *I am in the image and likeness of God—¶*
>
> *I am a part of His Being, and He is a part of mine—¶*
>
> *The God-qualities in me enable me to achieve relief from inner tensions of body, emotions and mind—¶*
>
> *I am in the Infinite Light, and the Infinite Light is in me—¶*

THE ONE RULE FOR A NEW LIFE

Can the Supreme Intelligence direct the affairs of your life? It can . . . if allowed to do so. It can function through your mind.

Although there are numerous differences of opinion concerning the mind, it is generally agreed that it functions at more than one level. Each segment of mind directs the activities which occur at its level and all are blended into an operative whole.

Broadly speaking, there are levels both below and above the normally conscious level of your mind. Below is the subconscious which seems principally to direct the involuntary functions of your body and emotional reactions. Above is the supraconscious. Many insist that this mind segment devises master plans to be carried out by the normally conscious level, and that it is the repository in which is stored the remarkable insight which so frequently flashes into the life of the genius.

If the Supreme Intelligence is to direct your affairs, it must operate through these levels of your mind. Perhaps some day the scientist will explain how this is accomplished through the interblending of force fields emanating from the Infinite Mind and yours. Until then you will be helped in your affairs if you will act upon the principle that the Infinite Mind and your mind can be brought into harmonious relationship through the Inner Way.

The qualities of the Infinite Mind can be impregnated upon your mind whenever you establish the proper conditions. The basic essential is that you create a sense of rapport between your Self and God.

Around you is a Great Mind that can furnish guidance, either realized or unrealized, in all the important affairs of your life. When you calm your mind it becomes susceptible to the influence of the Infinite Mind. When you direct your attention inward your conscious mind partially drops its awareness of the surrounding world of material things and becomes attuned to the superior world of ideas and resplendent concepts. It gains a penetrating insight which it does not normally express.

The subconscious segment of your mind begins expressing on a new level. It directs the involuntary functions of your body and

THE INNER WAY

emotional responses with a greater awareness of your immediate needs. Its duties are performed with a new faithfulness and sense of responsibility.

The supraconscious finds a cleared channel to express itself. It becomes responsive to higher principles and subtler nuances of life's cosmic currents, and it filters its promptings into your consciousness with recognizable mental declarations.

You will discover yourself drawn into situations and associations which contribute to your progress and well being. Even the wisest of mystics cannot explain precisely how this is accomplished. He only knows it does occur. And you can make the same startling and satisfying discovery for yourself by traveling the Inner Way.

THE INNER WAY

The Inner Way to Stabilize Your Life

Let your mind be still. Let your heart be still. Mentally sever your connection with the world and its turmoil. Establish your connection with the organizing and stabilizing quality of the Infinite Mind.

Let there be manifest in your life that spiritual essence which emanates from the One Great Source of Life. Let there be manifest in your affairs that irridescent light which radiates from the One Great Source of light.

The three elements of your mind become endowed with orderliness and harmony. Normal consciousness, subconscious and supraconscious become compatible with one another and with Divine will and purpose. They operate in accordance with Divine plan.

Let these be your thoughts:

> *While my mind and heart are at rest*
> *I am becoming a stabilized center*
> *of spiritual consciousness—¶*

> *While my mind and heart are at rest*
> *I am becoming aware of the God*
> *Presence in me—¶*

> *The God Presence brings orderliness*
> *and stability to every situation in*
> *my life—¶*

> *I am in the Infinite Light,*
> *and the Infinite Light is in me—¶*

THE INNER WAY

The Inner Way to Improve Your Life

Even the most orderly life occasionally has a way of becoming disorganized. When this happens to you, begin immediately to plan so that each activity of the day is assigned its proper place. In your plan include time for the Inner Way.

Disorganization results when the various elements of your Self are not functioning harmoniously. By turning to the Inner Way you are calming each element and bringing it into harmonious association with the other elements of your Self.

The alignment of every element of your being to the superior levels of life is your purpose at this moment. You focus upon this goal by turning your attention inward to the very center of your being. There you become conscious of a deep and eternal peace which the world of things cannot disturb. There you are immersed in a radiant, eternal Light.

Give place in your mind to these thoughts:

Within me . . . God is—¶

As the Divine Image, I live in His Spirit—¶

As the Divine Image, I walk in His Way—¶

Every element of my life is at peace—¶

*I am in the Infinite Light,
and the Infinite Light is in me—¶*

THE INNER WAY

The Inner Way to Material Progress

Through this inner attunement you have the opportunity of engaging in a personal spiritual activity which will influence your material affairs. They will be affected by and receive direction from the God Consciousness level of your life.

Let your mind become centered on the fact that it is permeated with Infinite Mind . . . your body is permeated with Divine Substance . . . your affairs are integrated with Divine Purpose.

Let your outer senses be calmed. Let your attention become fully oriented inwardly. Let your mind activate its awareness of the Divine Presence ... its understanding of Divine Consciousness ... its sense of Divine Power and Purpose.

Let these ideas become paramount in your consciousness:

> *The Divine Presence is fully known by my Spiritual Self—¶*
>
> *As I calm my physical senses this knowledge is communicated to my conscious mind—¶*
>
> *I thus provide the Divine Presence the opportunity of functioning in me and in every area of my life—¶*
>
> *I am in the Infinite Light, and the Infinite Light is in me—¶*

THE INNER WAY

EMPHASIZE YOUR BEST QUALITIES

Few people realize what their best qualities really are. Most everyone possesses unsuspected attributes which are never fully used. Whatever your best qualities may be, known or unknown, it is possible for you to emphasize them and express the fullest potential of which you are capable.

The Inner Way provides a method of bringing your finest features to the fore. It allows numerous inner inhibited impulses to rise to the surface of your life . . . to surge into expression instead of lying neglected below the surface of your consciousness.

THE INNER WAY

Practice the Inner Way as a restraining influence upon the negative aspects of your personality. It minimizes them, sublimates them to your better attributes, often destroys them completely.

Before you engage in any momentous activity, perhaps in your work or an important association with others, spend a few moments on the Inner Way through one of the attunement aids which follow. It will assure your expressing the best you possibly can in every situation you encounter . . . and in ordinary everyday living, too.

First it will negate inner conflicts and discords. Just as any living thing dies without food, so do your undesirable attributes lose their ascendency when denied the life force of constant expression. Even a few

THE INNER WAY

moments daily on the Inner Way withholds enough sustenance to deny life to most of the unwanted characteristics we all possess.

Then, because you have expressed your desire for their appearance, your creditable attributes will begin to declare themselves. You will discover that suddenly you begin to think, speak and act in a way which presents your best qualities.

You will notice that new thoughts and forceful inclinations burst into your conscious mind . . . and you will realize that they did not originate there but gushed from some higher wellspring of your Self.

Spontaneous impulses, which you will express in word and deed, arrive in your mind as unaccountably as the miracle of life itself. The long inhibited inner Self has at last been provided the opportunity of expression. Its barbed enclosure of the lower personality has been destroyed. It bounds into freedom aflame with pent up creative fire.

Your best qualities deserve the opportunity to be expressed. You cannot select one of them and say, "I am going to express this attribute today." Specific unforeseen situations too often call in vain for specific aspects of your Self which you may not even realize you possess. But they wait in readiness and will manifest themselves if you have opened the way for them. Your inner deeps contain an abundance of vigorous talents which will augment the skills you have acquired through experience and education. Call them forth through the Inner Way.

THE INNER WAY

The Inner Way to Right Decisions

Every day . . . almost every minute . . . you are making apparently automatic judgments and decisions without using your conscious mind. Driving your car, at your work, in your home and relationships with others these quite unconscious activities comprise a considerable portion of your life. They are often more important than are major decisions.

Consider for a moment the forces which influence these judgments and decisions. Are they stabilized in a harmonious and productive foundation? Do they stem from a sound spiritual basis?

It is possible for you to mold the nature

of your more or less automatic judgments and decisions according to your needs and desires. To shape them according to Divine plan. To fortify them with Divine purpose.

Make these statements as inner directives:

> *The involuntary and automatic activities of my mind and body are spiritually influenced for my good—¶*
> *As I become attuned to the Infinite my capacities for judgment and decision are enhanced with Divine qualities—¶*
> *All that I say and do will harmonize with and contribute to my progress—¶*
> *I am in the Infinite Light,*
> *and the Infinite Light is in me—¶*

THE INNER WAY

*The Inner Way to
Develop Your Talents and Skills*

There is that Superlative Quality within you which is Divine. Like an inner, hidden treasure it must be sought persistently. Yet the searching is neither frenzied nor difficult. Each state of inner composure you create brings you nearer its realization.

The talents and skills you already possess can be enhanced . . . lifted to a new peak of expression . . . emphasized so that a new pinnacle of productivity is gained.

Let your mind be focussed on the innermost depths of your being. Let it move easily into this more meaningful area of your Self. Let it become aware of the ma-

THE INNER WAY

jesty, the power, and the wisdom of the inner essences it meets. Let it be infused with these qualities to such a degree that they become an active force in your outer life as well as the inner.

Center your mind upon these ideas:

> *I am attuned to the God that resides within me—¶*
>
> *From the God within I receive all the qualities which will emphasize my better capacities—¶*
>
> *From the God within I receive the qualities which will increase the effectiveness of my talents and skills—¶*
>
> *I am in the Infinite Light, and the Infinite Light is in me—¶*

*The Inner Way to
Enhance your Personality*

If you accept the idea that God is present within you, then you must realize there are many times when His Presence is denied the opportunity of expression through you.

Personality clashes and the misery they cause can often be avoided if you will provide the Inner Presence the opportunity to become functional in your association with others.

At this moment invite the Divine Omnipresence to become predominantly manifest in your life.

Ask the Divine Omniscience to manifest as wisdom and understanding in your mind.

Request the Divine Omnipotence to flow into your life, and every circumstance thereof.

Let your mind become suffused with these ideas:

> *I accord the Indwelling Presence the place of prominence in my life—¶*
>
> *I accept the Indwelling Presence as an integral portion of my own being—¶*
>
> *I acclaim the Indwelling Presence as the predominating influence in my life, reaching through me into the lives of others—¶*
>
> *I am in the Infinite Light, and the Infinite Light is in me—¶*

THE OPEN DOOR
TO THE FATHER'S HOUSE

Where is God that you might speak with Him and receive His answer? In some other person? Behind the altar of church or synagogue? In an indefinite place in space? A Divine Being in any of these outer places cannot be known intimately.

But there is a way in which you may have a deep personal association with God. Go to the place where He really is, within your Self, and there hold communion with Him . . . have a personal experience with the Divine Person. It will be an experience so intimate, so intense, so profound that you will treasure it the rest of your days.

THE INNER WAY

Religion, of whatever name or form, is an expression of man's inner Self in which there should be personal participation by that Self. The inspiration of a formal religious service is important. But unfortunately such services do not always provide the personal individual activity which identifies you with the Divine Person. Whether you are a Christian, Jew, Moslem, Buddhist, Hindu, Taoist, or follower of any other religion, you can supplement the formal practices of your faith with the intimate association with the Deity provided by the Inner Way.

The nature of your spirit and the nature of the Divine Spirit are the same. This is both a simple truth and a mystery.

It is also an opportunity. It provides both the possibility and the basis of your association with the Divine Being.

Dissimilar qualities, the proverbial oil and water, are not compatible. But similar qualities may be blended. In fact, they may both exist in the same place at the same time. This is true of your spirit and the Divine Spirit . . . like qualities which exist in the same place at the same time.

Because they do reside together in the same house, the lesser is influenced by the greater whenever the two are in accord with one another. When you take the Inner Way you are associating the inner elements of your nature with the Divine Nature. The momentum of this activity is carried through into your outer life.

This does not mean that you will suddenly become a person without human frailties . . . that you are superior to the foibles of your still-human nature . . . that

THE INNER WAY

you give up living in the world of men and things. You will not suddenly become a robe-adorned prophet with flowing beard, uttering historic pronouncements. The world, its people and their material strivings, will remain in your sight.

But when you take the Inner Way, and your nature mingles on intrinsic terms with the Divine Nature...

It does assure you that you will tend a holy altar in the innermost sanctuary of your consciousness. That at this meeting place with the Infinite you will grow in wisdom and understanding. That the struggles of life lose their smothering impact and you see the way to conquer them. That, at last, you have come into the Light and the Light has become an intimate, ever-glowing element of your life.

THE INNER WAY

The Inner Way to Contact the Infinite

The presence of God may be known in a discernible manner. It may be intuitively perceived and inwardly felt . . . as tangibly as the outer senses present their information to your consciousness.

In deliberately chosen moments of quietness you may come to recognize the particular spiritual feeling which indicates your attunement to His Being . . . to His Presence within you.

Momentarily disassociate your consciousness from the outer world to the greatest extent possible. Travel the Inner Way till you establish firmly your association with the inner world. A sense of reality which is outside time and space will pervade your consciousness.

Let your mind become focussed upon these ideas:

Every attribute and quality of God is within me now—¶

These Divine aspects penetrate my being and my life—¶

Through my attunement with them I become elevated to a higher level of consciousness—¶

My entire being and all my affairs become spiritualized and Divinely directed—¶

I am in the Infinite Light, and the Infinite Light is in me—¶

THE INNER WAY

The Inner Way to the Power of the Infinite

Attunement to the Divine Essences of Life is a rare privilege all too often ignored. It is not the special province of holy man, sage and seer, but provides its benefits to all who will avail themselves of it. This opportunity is before you now.

To affirm the Divine Presence is the first and introductory step. To become aware of the Divine Presence is to carry the inner activity to a greater height. To allow the Divine Presence to function through you is to attain the zenith of spiritual expression.

When your consciousness becomes coincident with the Divine Consciousness you and God are one. When the life force in you flows in exact rhythm with the Universal Life Force then you are in God and God is in you. It is possible so to adjust yourself inwardly, in mind and body, that a state of complete rapport between you and God is created.

As you turn within, carry these thoughts with you:

I affirm the Divine Presence in my life—¶

I become aware of the Divine Presence within my being—¶

I authorize the Divine Presence to act through me in all my relationships and affairs—¶

I am in the Infinite Light, and the Infinite Light is in me—¶

The Inner Way to the Great Source of Life

In this sacred moment you have the privilege of acquiring a greater and more personal knowledge of the Infinite. Come to know the Great Source of Life as a definite Presence within your own being.

Begin now to feel the warmth of Divine Love as it enters your own heart . . . and from thence radiates to every portion of your Self . . . and then outward into the world.

Allow the power of creativity, and the virtue of understanding, to find their rightful places in your mind.

Invite every essence of the Infinite to

flow as a soothing and strengthening balm into your life.

Express these ideas in your mind:

> *I am becoming a center of light to which the Greater Light is attracted—¶*
>
> *I am creating a power of good through which the Greater Good becomes apparent—¶*
>
> *I am becoming an instrument of love through which the Greater Love is manifest—¶*
>
> *I am in the Infinite Light,
> and the Infinite Light is in me—¶*

CREATIVE COOPERATION WITH THE INFINITE

You are, basically, a creator. Whether in a physical sense in the creation of things, or in a mental sense in the creation of ideas, you are constantly engaged in a micro-cosmic facsimile of the cosmic activity... creation.

Most people are *imitators*. They do what others do. Those who have made an outstanding success of life are *originators*. They do something a little different, give their lives a unique direction even though they may be engaged in commonplace activities. Imitators are stunting their creative abilities. Originators are emphasizing one

THE INNER WAY

of the most treasured of all their potentialities.

If you would be an originator instead of an imitator, align yourself with life's creative currents. You must use a personal method of opening the creative flow from the inner reservoir of your own being.

Henry Ford took solitary walks in the woods till new ideas occurred to him. William James each day personally sharpened exactly thirteen pencils before he felt the creative inspiration. Tennyson repeated his own name over and over till he entered the mystic state of creativity. Each of these psychological attunement activities served to align these remarkable men with the outpouring essences of their own creative powers.

You can accomplish the same objective

THE INNER WAY

through using the inner attunement aids which follow. You can achieve noteworthy improvement in your creative expressions by establishing the creative atmosphere in your consciousness through the Inner Way. Aligning the source of your own creativeness with Infinite creativeness provides the generating impulse which starts the flow from within.

Even prosaic and apparently routine occupations provide you with opportunities to be creative. Relationships with others present possibilities for your creative talents to be expressed. The arrangement of your home, your personal attire, music, art, literature, the field of entertainment, education . . . the list of endeavors in which creativeness may be expressed is limitless.

Every aspect of your life is subject to en-

THE INNER WAY

richment and a new vision when approached through the inwardly induced atmosphere of creativity.

So before engaging in any activity which has previously seemed dull and routine, spend a few moments journeying within. Your mind will be refreshed by its contact with the Infinite Mind. An enlightened vision of your efforts will appear on the horizon of your consciousness. The sparkle and vitality of a fresh approach to even the most commonplace tasks will contribute new meaning to your life.

New, different, even constructively daring ideas will occur to you. Your thoughts will bear the scintillating stamp of cosmic creativity . . . gained through the Inner Way.

THE INNER WAY

The Inner Way to Creative Work

Between you and the Infinite there exists a usually dormant connection. This association may be activated according to your desire, your will, and the ability you have acquired through regularly engaging in the Inner Way.

Let your consciousness turn to the inner Path of Light, and along this hallowed Way discover your affinity with the Creative Deity. Let your consciousness find its own wholeness in this association with the Divine Consciousness. Let your Self merge with the Divine Self.

Let the realization of your union with the Infinite permeate every portion of your

THE INNER WAY

being . . . and extend outward into every activity of your life.

Grant a permanent place in your mind to these thoughts:

> *I become associated with the Divine Being in completely harmonious attunement—¶*
>
> *I become infused with Divine Creative Essences—¶*
>
> *These Essences encompass my Self and flood throughout my life and work as a billowing flow of Light—¶*
>
> *I am in the Infinite Light, and the Infinite Light is in me—¶*

The Inner Way to Creative Ideas

To be truly creative your mind must function at its highest capacity. Its supraconscious and intuitive elements must be freed from the inhibiting factors of the normal sense world.

The inward act of attunement to the Infinite is the most essential inner activity in which you may engage. It is an activity which concentrates every element of your mind upon their creative functions. It disengages you from temporal limitations and enfirms your association with constructive creative currents.

By the direction of your will you release yourself from the attractions of the imitative world and become imbued with the creative fire of the originative world.

You become aware of, and your mental nature harmoniously unites with, the creative power of the Universal Mind.

Let your attention be centered upon these thoughts:

I am one with the Infinite—¶

The Divine Essence permeates every portion of my being and is especially centered in my mind—¶

The Divine Creative Impulse motivates every act of my life—¶

*I am in the Infinite Light,
and the Infinite Light is in me—¶*

THE INNER WAY

*The Inner Way to
Creative Self-Expression*

In the inner spiritual atmosphere you create, it is possible for your consciousness to become infused with the harmonizing and strengthening radiation which has its source in life's Divine Impulse.

As you become outwardly calm, and inwardly at peace, you are attuned directly to the permeating Essence of God.

This is a hallowed moment of attunement with the Deity. This is a moment of spiritual realization. This is a moment of inner adjustment to the highest concept of Divinity to which you can now attain.

THE INNER WAY

This is a moment in which you *feel* the creative Presence of God in your Self.

Fix your mind upon these ideas:

I am in the presence of God . . . and God is present in me—¶

Every element of my consciousness is prepared to act in accord with Divine Principle—¶

Every element of my consciousness is prepared to act with an awareness of the Divinity which is within me—¶

I am in the Infinite Light, and the Infinite Light is in me—¶

ORGANIZE YOUR INNER LIFE

There are many who can skillfully organize world wide commercial enterprises but leave their own inner life in chaos. They comprise the world's unhappiest people.

However deftly you may coordinate home or business affairs, if the inner house is not in order you are the victim of the world's most tragic illness . . . unhappiness. Outer circumstances are nearly always accused as the cause of this malady. However, the fact remains that the outward stresses can be counteracted when the inner life is in the pattern of orderliness.

When your life becomes correlated with the Greater Life through the Inner Way, subtle influences begin to calm the inner disturbances which destroy your happiness. Relaxing muscular tensions in face and midriff are the outer signs which indicate that inner processes are forging a new character which is coordinate with essences of your divine Self.

Remember, first, that you are not a beggar at the rear door of life, pleading for a few crumbs of occasional satisfaction. You are the steward of an unparalleled treasury of riches which all the money and power in the world cannot wrest from you. All the deepest attributes you possess are safe from seizure. But as long as this treasure remains untouched by yourself . . . as long as you do not systemize the elements of your inner household . . . it remains buried and worthless.

THE INNER WAY

Your personal treasure, lustrous jewels of poise, contentment, joy and a thousand others . . . jewels of the spirit . . . may be radiantly expressed when you begin functioning from the inner instead of the outer Self. But this way of life is not accomplished by a feat of magic. You are not a genie in an Arabian Nights fairytale. You are a human being who possesses divine qualities which must be activated.

Your personal efforts are required. And the agency of your effort is the Inner Way. This is the method of arranging inner elements in correlation with outer requirements for truly successful living. This is the method of displaying your personal treasures to your own advantage, to the improvement of all your affairs, to the brightening of minds and the warming of hearts.

THE INNER WAY

Do you wish to be calm in the face of disturbances in business or personal relationships? Do you wish to discover a rich oasis of peace and happiness in the desert of problems and confusions? Do you wish to maintain orderly equilibrium in hurricanes of disorder?

Turn, then, to the Inner Way. Let your consciousness dip deeply into your inner treasures and carry them to the surface of your life. Open the corridor which provides easy passage to the attributes which will fashion anew the pattern of life you now follow. Let the inner attributes dissipate the outer convulsions which disorganize and confuse . . . and in their place establish order and system, calmness and serenity, composure and tranquility.

THE INNER WAY

The Inner Way to Order

When the Self of man and the Being of God are united, the result is a supreme state of inter-existence in which all that is part of one becomes also a part of the other.

Then if you would possess and express any of the qualities of Godhood, it is expedient for you so to organize your inner Self that it blends into, and becomes one with, the Divine Pattern.

You may accomplish this now as you turn to a momentary state of complete inner awareness . . . and as you become conscious of the inner Self as being in the Divine Image.

All that is in the Divine Pattern may also

be found in you. The orderliness of the Divine Pattern is also inherent in you, awaiting your outer expression of it.

Let your mind entertain these thoughts:

> *In this moment of inner spiritual attunement I become conscious of my true Self—¶*
>
> *I discover my Self to be in the Divine Image—¶*
>
> *I discover my Self to be of the Divine Image—¶*
>
> *I direct my Self to be in the Divine Pattern—¶*
>
> *I am in the Infinite Light, and the Infinite Light is in me—¶*

THE INNER WAY

The Inner Way to Harmony

Let the next few moments be dedicated to the spiritualizing of your consciousness . . . to the acceptance of the Infinite Consciousness into your own.

In the spiritualized state of mind which you are creating, the Infinite Consciousness assumes a more prominent place in every aspect of your life. It places the imprint of the Divine Presence upon you . . . upon every circumstance of your life . . . upon every activity in which you engage . . . upon each of your life objectives.

The essences of creativeness, accomplishment of purpose, proper and harmonious

THE INNER WAY

direction of life, all become active ingredients in your life expression.

Welcome these ideas into your mind:

In my mind the Infinite Consciousness finds a meetingplace with life—¶

Through my brain the Infinite Consciousness acts upon my body—¶

Through my entire being the Infinite Consciousness acts upon all the situations with which I am concerned—¶

*I am in the Infinite Light,
and the Infinite Light is in me—¶*

THE INNER WAY

The Inner Way to Serenity

There is as real an inner world as an outer. And it is through this inner world that you become attuned to, and aligned with, that Supreme Being to which, in various languages and forms, men have given the name God.

Whatever the name or form, God is the embodiment of an orderly life. Calmness and serenity are constant qualities which are part of Him, and part of you.

Emanating from the Supreme Being is a Divine Essence, a Light, which permeates the universe and every portion thereof. To make this Light actively your own, to receive its unnumbered benefits, center yourself in the current of the Divine Essence. Let every portion of your Being be bathed in it and influenced by it.

Focus your attention upon these ideas:

I am uniting my Self with the emanating Essence of God—¶

This spiritual Essence cleanses me of all inner disturbances and establishes calmness and serenity within—¶

It tempers the intemperate portions of my Self—¶

It strengthens the weaker portions of my Self—¶

As it becomes a part of my being, I become more truly and completely a part of God—¶

*I am in the Infinite Light,
and the Infinite Light is in me—¶*

FEEL THE DYNAMIC PRESENCE

Most people have been vaccinated with just enough superficial religion to prevent their ever achieving a deep and penetrating case of true supersensible understanding and experience. They never realize what they can accomplish when the Divine Dyname animates their lives.

Perhaps this is man's basic error in life . . . that he segregates and disconnects himself from the Divine.

God is too often presented as a separate entity, completely apart from the man who is supposed to know Him intimately. Your psyche and God's soul are too frequently considered as having opposite and contrary

THE INNER WAY

centers, when in truth a mystic union holds them in a common bond. Both transcend the dimensional world, yet both are centered upon the same point in space and time.

Is it possible for you to feel the impetus of God's Presence? Every person who has ever had a true spiritual experience has stated that it not only can be perceived but that it also provides an exhilirating impulse to every act of life which follows.

If you have not yet encountered this dynamic Presence of God . . . if you have not felt its powerful surge into expression through your life . . . then you have missed one of life's rare privileges, and the situation should be rectified as quickly as possible.

But how? We are often exhorted to have

an experience in association with God, though we are seldom told how it is to be accomplished. The mystics of every religious climate insist that the penetrating Light of God is known through the Inner Way.

A few moments of quietness on frequent occasions. A momentary refusal to heed the signals of the physical senses.

A determined control of the flitting mind through concentration on a specific objective.

A projection of the consciousness to its inmost center.

These are the elements of spiritual attunement which enable you to feel the Divine Presence.

Then the Presence begins to function

through you. Its impulse motivates your life in previously unconsidered directions. Wonders are performed. A divine animation enables you to see and understand and do that which previously would have been impossible.

The handiwork of the Presence operating through you becomes easily observable. An unaccountable vitality begins to appear. A subtle current of purposeful direction flows through your business affairs. Personal relationships are enhanced with deeper meaning.

The Presence is dynamic . . . and you feel it in every fibre and element of your being. You have achieved one of life's greatest goals when you feel the Dynamic Presence . . . the Presence that is already within you.

THE INNER WAY

The Inner Way to the Infinite Presence

This is the time to commune with the Infinite Being . . . to let your thoughts transcend the normal limitations with which they struggle and become transfixed upon the Infinite level of life.

You approach the Infinite level of life where your Self and the Infinite Being function in unison. This is the time to feel your Self in the presence of God. This is the time to feel the Presence of God in your Self.

Direct your consciousness to enter the Divine Light. Allow the Divine Light to enter your consciousness.

THE INNER WAY

Follow these attunement thoughts:

The outer world is stilled . . . and the inner world assumes the place of prominence in my mind—¶

The lower world comes to rest . . . only the higher world within is active—¶

I inwardly sense a new state of consciousness . . . a rapport . . . with the Infinite Presence—¶

The warmth and vitality of the Infinite Presence pervade every portion of my being—¶

I am in the Infinite Light, and the Infinite Light is in me—¶

THE INNER WAY

*The Inner Way to
Let God Act Through You*

God is an Inner Presence which can be inwardly felt. And from the inner sensing of this Presence you derive generous quantities of the attributes of which God is constituted.

Through focusing your attention on the God-Center within, you inaugurate a flow of those Divine Essences which are essential to the harmonious functioning of your life. The Divine Dyname acts through you as its instrument of expression.

Direct your mind to comprehend the Presence of God. Perceive the inner God-Quality which is an eternally resident por-

THE INNER WAY

tion of your being. Experience the reality of the inner Infinite.

Endow your mind with these ideas:

> *I realize that God is within me and all my affairs—¶*

> *I sense the Infinite Presence as part of my being . . . and my life . . . and all my activities—¶*

> *I know God—¶*

> *I know God acts through me—¶*

> *I am in the Infinite Light, and the Infinite Light is in me—¶*

THE INNER WAY

*The Inner Way to
Receive the Dynamic Infinite Spirit*

For a few moments engage in the process of functioning through the inner and higher dimensions of your Self. Let your thoughts turn inward and away from the outer physical world. Let them discover, and explore, the inner spiritual world.

Acquire the realization that it is here you meet with the Infinite. Through these inner and higher dimensions you comprehend your oneness with God. You objectify the purposes of that oneness.

You accept into your being those qualities which flow from the Great Source of Life into the focal point of life which you are . . . a dynamic focal point through which the Infinite expresses itself.

Give place in your consciousness to these thoughts:

> *I momentarily turn away from that area of my mind which is directed toward material and physical activities—¶*
> *I turn toward that area of my mind which is concerned with spiritual realization—¶*
> *In this higher dimension of my Self I meet with God—¶*
> *I accept the qualities which flow from the Great Source into me . . . and which thus become objectified in my life—¶*
> *I am in the Infinite Light,*
> *and the Infinite Light is in me—¶*

THE INNER WAY

THE KEY TO YOUR DESIRES

A double lock in most lives prevents the Infinite from manifesting in them. But the keys are available.

We have long been told that God is looking for something evil in us in order to inflict the appropriate punishment. If man is a Divine creation this is a poor commentary of God's ability.

Would it not seem considerably nearer the logical core of the matter to say that God is looking for the good in us in order to emphasize it?

Having this fact in mind is one key to letting the Infinite manifest through you. The best inner properties you possess are

THE INNER WAY

the very qualities which enable the Infinite Light to shine in your life and into the lives of others. Always remember this fact. Do not dwell on your lesser attributes. Concentrate on the higher and better.

There is another aspect of the Infinite which is seldom understood. God does not overwhelm you and assume any authority in your life without an invitation. The attributes of the Infinite do not become suprafunctional on your behalf until you make the request and prepare the way. This is the second key.

Making the request and preparing the way are such close partners in spiritual affairs that one activity on your part fulfills both requirements . . . practice the Inner Way.

THE INNER WAY

The Infinite can manifest through you whenever you provide the opportunity. You can begin the process in the next few moments. The prime essential is to arouse and stimulate the deepest center of your Self . . . the terminal through which God activity transpires. This inner point where you and the Infinite meet is normally dormant through disuse. When it becomes the object of your attention it is quickened into purposeful activity.

Inner attunement clears the way. It activates long unused lines of communication between the Infinite and your normal mind, between the Infinite and your body, between the Infinite and all your affairs. This is especially noticeable when occasional intuitive sparks of wisdom and understanding beyond your normal expectation enlighten your mind. These brief intervals of higher dimensional thinking will provide you with ample evidence of both the unlimited capacity of your mind and the manifesting presence of the Infinite therein.

You occupy space. The Infinite occupies interspace. That is how close the Infinite is to you. You and the Infinite are conjoined in the same electronic force field. There is no reason why the Infinite cannot manifest through you except your unwillingness to allow it.

So clear the way now. Become charged with the promptings of the Infinite. Receive Divine directives which are personalized for your particular life. Let the Infinite manifest through you.

THE INNER WAY

The Inner Way to Success in Business

This is a moment of spiritual realization . . . when the spiritual elements of your being exert their influence . . . when you become aware of the peace and harmony and strength that progress outward from the eternal springs of life within . . . when you realize that the Spirit of God is part of the actual substance of your life.

This is a moment when the wisdom and power of the Infinite begin to make themselves known in your material enterprises. Through the focal point of your consciousness they radiate into the substance of each of your affairs.

You function as an extension of the Infinite. And the qualities of the Infinite function as an extension of you. Each of your material affairs becomes permeated with those qualities.

Let your mind entertain these thoughts:

> *I center my consciousness upon the act of attunement with the Infinite—¶*
>
> *The Spirit of God, acting from within my own being, urges a spiritual approach to my life, its problems, its triumphs—¶*
>
> *The Spirit of God is individualized in me—¶*
>
> *The Spirit of God manifests through me—¶*
>
> *I am in the Infinite Light,
> and the Infinite Light is in me—¶*

THE INNER WAY

*The Inner Way to
Success in Personal Relationships*

As you attempt to quicken the inner center where you and the Infinite meet, acquire a realization of the fact that there are cosmic patterns which you do not understand in your normal consciousness. These cosmic patterns bear a relationship to your personal needs and desires.

Inwardly request that the realization of your needs and desires will be furthered through attunement with life's cosmic patterns. Lift yourself to the highest possible state of spiritual realization through the Inner Way of attunement.

As you enter this higher plane of consciousness let its atmosphere be indelibly impressed upon your mind. Preserve a remembrance of this exalted state to carry with you in all your personal relationships with others.

Center your attention upon these thoughts:

> *In the inner quietness, the Voice of the Infinite speaks silently but surely in my mind—¶*
>
> *In the calmness of this moment Infinite Love saturates my heart—¶*
>
> *Infinite Love flows through my entire being . . . and through me into the life of everyone I meet—¶*
>
> *I am in the Infinite Light, and the Infinite Light is in me—¶*

THE INNER WAY

*The Inner Way to
Success in Spiritual Growth*

As an activity of inner spiritual expression, unite with God . . . the Infinite Light . . . the Infinite Wisdom . . . the Infinite Power.

Let your mind become calmed and organized. Direct it to attain a state of spiritual attunement, devoid of attachments to the physical world.

As you approach this state you become aware of your entire being as a center of light. It is a center into which the Divine Light is being directed. It is a center into which God-Power is being absorbed. It is a center through which Divine Knowledge is expressing.

Dwell upon these thoughts:

God-Power is within me . . . within my body and within my mind—¶

The Infinite Life is always a part of my finite life—¶

My mind is conditioned by the Infinite Mind—¶

The Infinite Mind expresses itself through my mind—¶

I am in the Infinite Light, and the Infinite Light is in me—¶

TAP THE ETERNAL RESOURCES

In removing the cloak from nature's atomic secrets, science discovered that the old proverb, "Seeing is believing," is a gross untruth. That man must believe in things he cannot see, and that subtle and invisible influences wield a tremendous power in his life, are incontrovertable facts.

Science states that the constitution of the universe could more truthfully be considered musical than material. That, in effect, the basis of the universe is not matter, as was long supposed, but sound. What a remarkable validation of the ancient mystics who, without any scientific knowledge whatever, maintained that the holy sound,

THE INNER WAY

"The Word," was the beginning and the basis of all things.

But let us make a personal application of this idea to your life . . . especially your immediate needs at this or any other moment. Perhaps a tragedy has befallen you. Or a sorrow encumbers you. Or the prospect or actuality of material failure plagues you. Or illness and pain trouble you. Or disrupted personal relationships distress you. Or you have fallen heir to any other of the thousands of afflictions and vexations which torment the human mind and emotions.

Are there eternal resources upon which you may call for aid? Is it possible for you to obtain personal title to them? It is . . . through the Inner Way.

Let us return for a moment to science's

concept that the basic nature of the universe is sound rather than matter. Each object in the universe, through each of its atoms, emits its own harmony. The Infinite radiates a melody. Being in the image of the Infinite you render precisely the same melody, but in a different key. Thus, to become aligned with the Infinite is simply to change your key to coincide with that of the Infinite. This is accomplished through the Inner Way.

As you turn within in the process of inner attunement you are changing the entire trend of your life. In that heightened state of consciousness you become infused with all the resources which are resident in the Infinite. The capacities to meet life's problems, however strenuous, inflow into your being during those moments when the

THE INNER WAY

melody of your life and the melody of the Infinite actually are one.

The inner, latent features of the Infinite which have been dormant in you are activated in all their strength to cushion you against the blows you receive, to enable you to move forward forcefully in spite of hindrances and limitations.

You possess your own undreamed of resources which, when united with those of the Infinite, provide you with an extraordinary aptitude for withstanding life's buffetings . . . and for making the most of life's opportunities.

The more you draw upon the eternal resources the greater quantities of their endless supply do you receive. Turn now to the Inner Way and receive the unlimited assistance which the eternal resources can provide you.

THE INNER WAY

The Inner Way to Mental Alertness

Quietness of body and mind enable you to become inwardly attuned to the harmony of the Infinite, the divine resonance of life, and to draw upon all its resources. So for a few moments let your body and mind be stilled.

Let there be an opening of the Inward Way . . . the inner channels through which the Infinite Consciousness involves with your conscioussess . . . a blending of two streams of thought into one comprehensive current.

Let there be an inner realization that the Infinite provides strength and wisdom for all your activities and needs. Make a

THE INNER WAY

direct inner statement that you are now drawing upon these resources . . . particularly those which will contribute to alerting your mental capacities to their fullest possible potential.

Let these thoughts occupy your mind:

In this moment I begin to comprehend my oneness with the Infinite—¶

The reality of that oneness is inwardly intensified—¶

The Infinite Presence centers in my consciousness—¶

I draw upon the inner Infinite for the mental resources which will fulfill my need—¶

I am in the Infinite Light, and the Infinite Light is in me—¶

THE INNER WAY

The Inner Way to Physical Strength

For a few moments attune yourself to the inner presence of the Infinite. Move inwardly toward the realization that you are a part of the Divine Life, and the Divine Life is a part of you.

Realize that in inner quietness and momentary seclusion from the outer world you find the residence place of the Most High . . . that all the strength therein may be made part of your own life.

Divine Life, and all the promise it holds for you, seeks to fulfill your inner desires . . . to give you strength, to clarify your purpose in life, to motivate you outwardly toward the realization of that purpose.

THE INNER WAY

Let these thoughts abide in your mind:

Inwardly I stand before the altar of the Most High—¶

The emanations from that altar permeate my entire being—¶

I receive all the essences of the Divine Life—¶

I accept their strength and retain it henceforth as a substantial portion of my own life—¶

I am in the Infinite Light, and the Infinite Light is in me—¶

The Inner Way to Emotional Stability

The world of the Unseen is your greatest resource. From it you may obtain healing for body and mind, inner fortitude to bolster your qualities of character, intuitive guidance in the principal affairs of your life and numberless other treasures.

This higher spectrum of life may be approached at any time and any place. However, among the most effective conditions for placing yourself under the influence of this higher and stabilizing spectrum are quiet moments of inner attunement.

Inwardly now, visit the world unseen, real and eternal . . . the world of vibrant, stabilized life . . . the world around and

THE INNER WAY

within you and all the circumstances of your life.

Calmly apply your mind to these thoughts:

My objective senses are stilled and my inner senses become active—¶

Essences from the invisible source of supply fill every portion of my being . . . calming . . . easing tensions—¶

The inner presence of God calms me—¶

The inner power of God heals me—¶

I am in the Infinite Light, and the Infinite Light is in me—¶

MAKE YOUR LIFE PRODUCTIVE

Do you want to accomplish more than you seem able to at present? And in less time? The inner Infinite will help you do so.

The Infinite is not only transcendent; it is immanent. It is nearer than hand to glove. It operates from within to help you express a more productive life both materially and spiritually.

The Infinite will help you achieve more and understand more in life, but you must create the necessary conditions. You must make your contribution to the process. Do so through the Inner Way.

When the Divine Being was bringing order out of chaos "I was harmonizing with Him," said the compiler of the Book of Proverbs. Becoming aware of and attuned to your own spirit is the method of becoming aware of and attuned to Divine Spirit . . . of harmonizing with the Infinite.

As the lesser thinks of the greater it becomes infused with the characteristics of the greater. As you think of the Infinite an influx of the qualities composing the Infinite flows into your mind and body . . . indeed into all the affairs in your life. So the essential necessary for actualizing a more productive life is that your thoughts be directed to the channel through which a productive life is made possible.

Curb your wandering faculties of mind. Direct them to the inner point of contact with the Infinite.

If you wish to be more productive . . .

if you wish to accomplish more, learn more, do more . . . then open the way to the organizing, vitalizing influence of the Infinite. It is no easy task that has been set before you. To control the meandering mind and keep it constant on a state of inner attunement for just a few moments seems easy. Actually it is a rigid discipline. But perseverance and practice offer rich dividends, not only in an awareness of the Infinite inflowing into your life but also in new mental alertness.

In using these inner attunement aids it often helps to think of the Infinite as becoming personified in you . . . as a real person that in some mystic way is yourself and all your attributes magnified a hundred thousand times. This Inner Person will help you think with keen perception.

THE INNER WAY

It will help you organize your mind and your time. It will add an adroitness to your efforts far beyond your normal capacities. It will help arrange your affairs in their proper relationship to the objectives of your life.

So before practicing any of the attunement aids which follow, curb your wandering faculties of mind. Collect them and direct them to the inner point of contact with the Infinite. As you do so, firmly implant in your consciousness the fact that this inner attunement is for the specific purpose of increasing the effectiveness of your life . . . for enhancing the alertness and efficiency of your mind.

THE INNER WAY

The Inner Way to Improve Your Memory

Your mind begins to function in a different way when you deliberately associate it with the Infinite Mind.

It puts aside undue concern for the transient . . . severs its adherence to the constantly changing and always deteriorating elements of physical substance . . . asserts its life, vitality and constancy.

Association with the Infinite Mind enables your mind to function on a new level of alertness and efficiency. Enables it to become steadfast in purpose and direction, and to function in harmony with the Infinite. Enables it to retain its experiences.

THE INNER WAY

So consolidate the association of your mind with the Infinite Mind.

Direct your consciousness to consider these ideas:

Under the direction of my will my mind becomes harmoniously attuned with Infinite Mind—¶

Every portion of my mind becomes permeated with the elements of Infinite Mind—¶

The Infinite Mind and my mind function as a single unit, harmoniously moving toward the same goal—¶

The ability of my mind to retain a clear memory of essentials is now being emphasized—¶

*I am in the Infinite Light,
and the Infinite Light is in me—¶*

THE INNER WAY

The Inner Way to Gain Important Goals

The material way of life is an obviously important portion of our existence. Often we become so involved in gaining our material goals that we overlook the contribution which the spiritual impulse can give to all material undertakings. Pursuing the material way of life properly requires arranging states of balance between it and life's spiritual essences.

Just as no material idea is expressed by your mind unless you allow it or deliberately will it, neither will essential balancing spiritual ideas be expressed unless you allow it or deliberately will it.

The next few moments should be dedicated to this process. To endowing material desires with spiritual qualities. To creating an inner spiritual atmosphere in which your material objectives may be infused with spiritual vitality.

Center your attention upon these ideas:

The entire atmosphere of my physical and material life is being endowed with spiritual qualities—¶

These are the qualities of God which are manifest in me because He is in me—¶

These qualities spiritualize every aspect of my life, even my most material endeavors—¶

*I am in the Infinite Light,
and the Infinite Light is in me—¶*

THE INNER WAY

*The Inner Way to
Awaken the Whole Person*

The life that is centered only upon material things is narrow and limited. Actually it is but half a life. It feeds only the outer man and allows the inner man to starve.

At this moment you have the opportunity of increasing the dimensions of your life. New depths of consciousness and new heights of realization await the directive of your mind in order to be realized.

These greater dimensions of life lie within you. Your faculty of inner sensing makes you aware of them. Turning your consciousness to this inner sensing is entering the "holy of holies" and coming into the presence of God.

Let these thoughts be uppermost in your mind:

> *Awareness of the temporal world momentarily dissolves from my consciousness—¶*
>
> *Realization of the eternal world enters my mind—¶*
>
> *In this eternity domain I come under the influence of the presence and power of God—¶*
>
> *My consciousness becomes consistent with His . . . my desires coincide with His . . . my life is expressed in accordance with His—¶*
>
> *I am in the Infinite Light,*
> *and the Infinite Light is in me—¶*

THE INNER WAY

THE END OR

THE BEGINNING?

As a final word may I remind you that nothing is final—

Even death is a birth into a new dimension of life. In everything you do the end of one experience is always the beginning of another. The stream of life and all your experiences in it is never-ending . . . each instant the child of all that has gone before and the parent of all that is to follow.

Considered in this light, discouragement, failure and illness are seen as merely temporary states which need only have their direction reversed to become their exact opposites of enthusiasm, success and health.

I suggest that you cease looking for "conclusions" in your life and look always for "commencements."

Instead of saying, "I wish this condition would end," why not say, "Through this condition is a way to a new beginning."

Let your mind find new dimensions to explore through inner association with the Infinite. Let the Infinite Way become your personal way to a life that is full and rich ... and enhanced with all the high qualities you possess.

The End?
Or the Beginning?
Only You Can Decide!

A Message from Astara

Astara makes this book available to you in the belief that it will contribute to your life on its various important levels: physical, emotional, intellectual, and spiritual.

Actually, we consider this volume to be an extension of the teachings contained in Astara's series of mystical studies known as *Astara's Book of Life*. The lessons comprising the *Book of Life* are distributed on a world-wide basis only to members of Astara.

Astara was founded in 1951 as a non-profit religious organization including the following concepts:

1. A center of all religions, oriented to mystical Christianity but accepting and teaching all religions as beneficial to humankind.
2. A school of the Ancient Mysteries, offering a compendium of the esoteric teachings of all ages.
3. A fraternity of all philosophies, coordinating many viewpoints of humankind and the interacting inner structures which unite us as one in the Infinite.
4. An institute of psychic research, with special attention directed to spiritual healing of physical, emotional and mental aspects, and to life before and after physical incarnation.

If these concepts interest you, you may wish to pursue the studies of *Astara's Book of Life* as have thousands of others in some ninety countries around the world.

To give you information about Astara, its teachings, and other possible services to you, we have prepared a treatise entitled *Finding Your Place in the Golden Age*. You may have it without cost or obligation. To obtain it, simply direct your request to:

>   The Registrar
>   Astara
>   800 W. Arrow Hwy.
>   Upland, Calif. 91786

Remembering

THE AUTOBIOGRAPHY OF A MYSTIC
By Earlyne Chaney

Earlyne Chaney whose quest for truth led through Hollywood to world-wide prominence as a teacher of mysticism.

REMEMBERING is ... a story of life after death ... and love beyond death ... the story of a quest for a love from a past life whose eyes haunted her dreams ... of contact with a Great Being from the Other Side whose influence brought illumination to one in search of Light.

Do you believe unseen beings guide our lives?

Do you believe unseen beings sometimes guide and guard those whose destiny is marked for greatness? *Remembering* tells of such a being — his appearance and his prophecy to a girl whose search for God led her away from orthodox religion and into mysticism ...

Do you believe in life after death?

Do you believe our loved ones can, under certain circumstances, return to bring solace and guidance to their bereft? *Remembering* tells of the pilot whose death in a plane crash changed the life of this same girl — how she turned from a career as a movie actress to search for the meaning of life and death and immortality. And how he returned to tell her he still lived ...

Cpt. Marvin Moore the pilot who pierced the veil of shadows to tell of continued life.

Do you believe you have lived before?

... and that you can dream dreams of the one whose love endured from the past? *Remembering* tells of the girl's lonely search for the beloved and how the pilot, from the Other Side of life, guided her to find the eyes that haunted her dreams.

This autobiography of a mystic is a true story of life from a humble beginning to a film career, then to eminence as one of today's outstanding authors of mystical teachings whose writings are sought by mystical seekers the world over.

Remembering by Earlyne Chaney is a life-changing experience. A journey through its pages is an upgoing path into the starmists of your own soul searchings, vague rememberings of other lives, other loves, other hopes, your own yet-to-be dreams.

Robert Chaney whose love, haunting her dreams of a long-ago life, guided her way into a new light.

"... a philosophically guided tour past the treasured milestones of memory in the romantically inspiring life of the modern mystic, Earlyne Chaney."
—Harold Sherman, author of *How to Make ESP Work for You* and *You Live After Death*

At your bookstore, or order from
Astara, Upland, CA 91786